The Urbana Free Library

To renew: call 217-367-4057
or go to *urbanafreelibrary.org*
and select "My Account"

What's the Issue?

WHO ARE REFUGEES?

By Joyce Jeffries

KidHaven PUBLISHING

Published in 2018 by
KidHaven Publishing, an Imprint of Greenhaven Publishing, LLC
353 3rd Avenue
Suite 255
New York, NY 10010

Designer: Seth Hughes
Editor: Katie Kawa

Photo credits: Cover (top), p. 5 Nicolas Economou/Shutterstock.com; cover (bottom) dinosmichail/Shutterstock.com; p. 4 Giannis Papanikos/Shutterstock.com; p. 6 Dan Kitwood/Getty Images; p. 7 (background) arsenisspyros/iStock/Thinkstock; p. 7 (sticky note) slav/iStock/Thinkstock; p. 8 Yuriy Boyko/Shutterstock.com; p. 9 Spencer Platt/Getty Images; p. 10 Keystone/Getty Images; p. 11 Gerry Cranham/Getty Images; p. 12 EDUARDO SOTERAS/AFP/Getty Images; p. 13 MUSTAFA MULOPWE/AFP/Getty Images; pp. 14, 15 Sumy Sadurni/Barcroft Images/Barcroft Media via Getty Images; p. 16 © istockphoto.com/AhmadSabra; p. 17 (left) a katz/Shutterstock.com; p. 17 (right) DANIEL LEAL-OLIVAS/AFP/Getty Images; p. 18 John Moore/Getty Images; p. 19 (left) Win McNamee/Getty Images; p. 19 (right) JEWEL SAMAD/AFP/Getty Images; p. 20 Jordan Pix/Getty Images; p. 21 © istockphoto.com/sadikgulec.

Library of Congress Cataloging-in-Publication Data

Names: Jeffries, Joyce, author.
Title: Who are refugees? / Joyce Jeffries.
Description: First Edition. | New York : KidHaven Publishing, [2018] |
  Series: What's the issue? | Includes index.
Identifiers: LCCN 2017036587| ISBN 9781534524330 (library bound book) | ISBN
  9781534525023 (6 pack) | ISBN 9781534525016 (pbk. book) | ISBN
  9781534524347 (eBook)
Subjects: LCSH: Refugees.
Classification: LCC HV640 .J44 2018 | DDC 305.9/06914–dc23
LC record available at https://lccn.loc.gov/2017036587

Printed in the United States of America

CPSIA compliance information: Batch #CW18KL: For further information contact Greenhaven Publishing LLC, New York, New York at 1-844-317-7404.

CONTENTS

Searching for Safety

People move from one country to another for many reasons. In many cases, they move because they want to. In other cases, they move because they have to. Their home is no longer safe, and they must leave to **protect** themselves and their families.

These people are refugees, and there are millions of them living all around the world today. Refugees hope to find safety in new places, but it's not always easy for them to escape and start over. However, there are many ways you can help refugees close to home and far away.

Facing the Facts 🔍

More than half of the world's refugees are children under the age of 18.

Many refugees travel a long way to find safety. They may walk for many miles or take crowded boats.

Refugee or Migrant?

Some people come to live in another country to better their lives. They do this by finding new jobs, going to school, or meeting up with family members. Their lives weren't directly **threatened** back home, and if they went back, they wouldn't be in danger. These people are known as immigrants, or migrants.

Migrants and refugees aren't the same. Refugees leave because of a direct threat to their safety. They feel they can't return home, and that's why they come to another country. Then, they apply for asylum, which is **legal** protection and other help given only to refugees.

Facing the Facts 🔍

The 1951 Refugee Convention is an agreement signed by countries around the world that spells out who refugees are and what their rights are. It only covered European refugees at first, but it was added to in 1967 to cover refugees from other countries.

Different Names for Different Groups

group	Who are they?
immigrants (migrants)	people who come to another country for reasons other than a direct threat to their lives
asylum seekers	people who are applying to be protected as refugees
refugees	people who have been forced to leave their home country because of a threat to their safety or their lives
internally displaced persons (IDPs)	people who have been forced to leave their home but stay in their country without protection from the 1951 Refugee Convention
returnees	refugees who return to their home country after it has become safe to do so

There are many groups of people who leave their homes for different reasons. Knowing the differences between them is important.

Why Do They Leave?

It's hard for refugees to leave their homes, and sometimes it's **dangerous**. However, it's more dangerous for them to stay. Refugees live in countries that are torn apart by war and other **violence**, which makes them afraid for their lives.

Some refugees live in countries where they face persecution, or unfair and unkind treatment because they're different from people in power. People are persecuted for their race, **religion**, country of birth, and many other reasons. Refugees have a good reason to believe they might die if they're not given asylum in another country.

8

Facing the Facts 🔍

There are 22.5 million refugees around the world, according to the United Nations (UN) Refugee Agency, which is a group that was formed to protect the rights of refugees and IDPs.

As of 2017, more than 5 million refugees have come from the Middle Eastern country of Syria. This country's civil war, which began in 2011, has killed millions of men, women, and children. It's also left millions homeless and afraid, seeking asylum in other countries.

Refugees Throughout History

Refugees have existed as long as people in power have tried to persecute or kill those who are different. For example, thousands of Jewish people became refugees in 1492, when they were forced to leave Spain because of their religious beliefs.

Political changes have also caused people to seek safety in other countries throughout history. In the 20th century alone, **revolutions** in Russia, Hungary, Cuba, and other nations forced millions from their homes. Breaking up pieces of land, such as taking away part of Palestine to create Israel in 1948, has also led to major refugee movements.

Facing the Facts 🔍

In 2016, only 5 percent of refugees came to the United States from Europe.

During World War II,
about 60 million people became refugees.
Many of these refugees were Jewish people
who were being persecuted during this time.

11

African and Asian Refugees

The refugee **crisis** in Syria has been called the worst refugee crisis since World War II, but Syria isn't the only place refugees come from. Afghanistan is another Middle Eastern country many people are forced to leave to stay safe. Wars have made that country very unstable and unsafe for many years.

Large numbers of refugees also come from African nations such as Somalia, South Sudan, and the Democratic Republic of the Congo. More refugees came to the United States from the Democratic Republic of the Congo than from any other country in 2016 and 2017.

Facing the Facts

In 2016, the United States took in refugees from 78 different countries.

An uprising in the Democratic Republic of the Congo began in 2016 and has led to deadly violence, children being armed as soldiers, and millions of people being forced from their homes.

Refugee Camps

Where do refugees live after they leave their homes? Many find safety and supplies at refugee camps not far from their home countries. Some refugees only stay at these camps for a short time. Others live there for years.

The camps provide refugees with food, water, health care, and places to sleep. They also have schools, and many have businesses run by refugees, such as bike repair shops. In large camps, there are more than 2,000 businesses providing goods and services to other refugees. Life in a refugee camp isn't easy, but for many, it's safer than the life they left behind.

Facing the Facts 🔍

As of 2017, the Bidi Bidi refugee camp in the African country of Uganda is the largest refugee camp in the world. More than 270,000 refugees stay at this camp.

The Bidi Bidi refugee camp, shown here, has become a safe place for people escaping South Sudan's deadly civil war.

Strong Feelings

Refugees leave their home countries seeking safety, but in some cases, other people are afraid refugees will make their own countries less safe. Some violent people who have sought asylum in countries such as Germany have carried out bombings and other attacks. These crimes have caused some people to see all refugees as possible **terrorists**.

Marches against refugees have been held around the world, but there have also been many gatherings in support of refugees. Although some people are afraid of refugees, others believe taking in refugees is the right thing to do.

Facing the Facts 🔍

As of April 2017, 57 percent of American voters believe Syrian refugees should be accepted into the United States.

People often feel strongly about refugees and their right to live among us. This is especially true for refugees from countries that practice the religion of Islam. Many terrorist attacks have been carried out by Islamic **extremists**, even though most people who practice this religion do not support this kind of violence.

A Threat?

Americans have often been opposed to letting big groups of refugees into the country. Today, national security plays a big part in the belief that we should keep refugees out rather than take them in. People believe keeping refugees from certain countries out will keep America safer.

In early 2017, President Donald Trump tried to ban all refugees from Syria. Although that ban was struck down by courts, a limit was placed on the total number of refugees allowed into the United States. Only 50,000 refugees were supposed to be allowed in 2017, and that number was reached in July.

Facing the Facts 🔍

The odds of a person being killed by a refugee in a terrorist attack in the United States is 1 in 3.6 billion.

Some Americans, such as President Donald Trump, support limiting the number of refugees allowed into the United States. Other Americans believe all refugees should be welcomed.

A Helping Hand

Many people work to help refugees stay safe and find new places to live. One of the most important groups created to help refugees is the UN Refugee Agency. It provides lifesaving services to refugees in 130 countries. Refugee children are also helped by UNICEF, which is a part of the UN that deals mainly with young people.

You can help refugees, too! Giving money to these groups is one way to help. You can also support businesses run by refugees in your community. It's good to help refugees feel at home in a new place.

Facing the Facts 🔍

The famous actress Angelina Jolie works with the UN to speak out about the hard times refugees face and to help them build better, safer lives.

WHAT CAN YOU DO?

Give money to groups that help refugees.

Be kind and welcoming to refugees in your school or neighborhood.

Write a letter to a refugee through the **CARE** website (after asking your parents or guardians).

Learn more about refugees.

Help groups in your community that aid refugees.

Support businesses run by refugees.

If you want to help refugees, it's easy to get started!

GLOSSARY

crisis: A hard and often unsafe situation that needs attention.

dangerous: Not safe.

extremist: A person who believes in or supports ideas that are very far from what people consider correct or reasonable.

legal: Relating to the law.

political: Relating to government and beliefs about how governments should work.

protect: To keep safe.

religion: A set of beliefs about a god or gods.

revolution: The overthrowing of a ruler or government by force.

terrorist: A person who uses violent acts to frighten people as a way of trying to achieve a political goal.

threat: The possibility that something bad or harmful could happen.

violence: The use of bodily force to hurt others.

FOR MORE INFORMATION

WEBSITES

"Kids, Refugees, Questions: 'What Is It Like to Have No Home?'"
www.theguardian.com/global/video/2016/dec/09/kids-refugees-questions-whats-it-like-to-have-no-home-video
This video features British children and young refugees asking and answering questions about their lives.

Searching for Syria
searchingforsyria.org/en
This interactive website, which was created by the UN Refugee Agency, answers common questions about the Syrian refugee crisis.

BOOKS

McCarney, Rosemary. *Where Will I Live?* Toronto, ON: Second Story Press, 2017.

Roberts, Ceri, and Hanane Kai. *Refugees and Migrants*. London, UK: Wayland, 2016.

Rodger, Ellen. *A Refugee's Journey from the Democratic Republic of the Congo*. New York, NY: Crabtree Publishing Company, 2017.

INDEX